BIG ENGLISH 1

T0385795

Mario Herrera • Christopher Sol Cruz

PUPIL'S BOOK

Contents

CLIL	Values	Phonics	I can...
Maths: Counting notebook, pencil case, pencil sharpener, tablet How many pencils have you got? I've got three pencils. **Project:** My Pencil Case poster	**Be polite.** Thank you. You're welcome. Please sit down.	**a, t, p, n** an, ant, at tan, tap pan, pant, pat nap	...name classroom objects. ...talk about the things I've got. ...be polite.
Social Science: Gender baby, boy, girl, man, woman This woman is my mum. This girl is my sister. This is my sister. **Project:** Family poster	**Help your family.** Can I help you? Yes, thank you. Please help me. OK. I can help you.	**i, s, b, d** in, is, it, pin sad, sit bad, bat dad, dip	...talk about my family. ...say how many brothers and sisters I've got. ...ask to help my family.
Science: The senses hear, see, smell, taste cake, flower, guitar, ice cream, photo I see with my eyes. I taste with my mouth. I hear with my ears. I smell with my nose. **Project:** My Senses poster	**Keep clean.** Wash with soap. Rinse with water. Dry your hands.	**e, c, g, m** pen, pet cap, cat gas, get, wig map, mat	...name parts of the body. ...talk about my senses. ...say how I keep clean.
Social Science: Weather and clothing cold, dry, hot, wet desert, jungle, mountains It's cold in the mountains. I'm wearing a jacket. **Project:** Clothes poster	**Respect all cultures.** They're wearing traditional clothes from Guatemala.	**o, k, ck** dog, on, pot kid, kit kick, neck, pick, sock	...say what people are wearing. ...talk about clothes. ...respect all cultures.
Art: Shapes circle, rectangle, square, triangle flat, houseboat, lighthouse, yurt **Project:** House Shapes poster	**Help at home.** He's washing the dishes. She's drying the dishes. She's cleaning her room. She's helping her parents.	**u, f, ff** run, sun, up fan, fog, fun off, puff	...talk about home activities. ...find and say shapes in homes. ...talk about helping at home.
Social Science: Baby animals calf, chick, kitten, puppy A baby chicken is called a chick. **Project:** Baby Animals poster	**Be kind to animals.** feeding, walking I'm feeding the chicks.	**r, h, j** red, rock, run hat, hen, hut jam, jet, job	...name animals and baby animals. ...talk about what animals are doing. ...say how to be kind to animals.
Science: Sweet and salty food biscuits, chips, chocolate, crisps, salt, sugar salty, sweet Crisps are salty. Chocolate is sweet. **Project:** Sweet and Salty Food poster	**Eat three meals a day.** I eat breakfast every day. I eat lunch every day. I eat dinner every day. I eat salad for lunch every day.	**l, ll, v, w** leg, let bell, doll, tall van, vet we, web, win	...talk about party food. ...ask and answer about what people have got. ...name sweet and salty food.
Art: Kites bird, butterfly, dragon, fish This kite looks like a fish. It's green. **Project:** Cool Kite	**Share your toys.** Sharing is fun! Here's my car. Let's share. Okay. Thank you!	**qu, x, y** quack, quick box, fox, ox, six yell, yes, yum	...name toys. ...say where something is. ...talk about sharing my toys.
P.E. Playground games hide and seek, hopscotch, tag climb, hop Let's play hide and seek. **Project:** Play Time poster	**Look after your body.** Get enough exercise. Get enough sleep. Get enough food and drink.	**ss, z, zz** kiss, mess, miss zap, zip buzz, fizz, jazz	...talk about actions people are doing. ...talk about games children play. ...say how I look after my body.

Welcome to Class!

1 Listen, look and say.

Listen. Ask and answer.

Hello! What's your name?

I'm Anna. What's your name?

I'm Sam. Goodbye!

Goodbye, Sam!

Listen and point.

Hello, pupils. I'm Mrs Smith. I'm your teacher.

Hello, Mrs Smith!

How are you, Tim?

I'm fine, thanks.

1

2

Look at 3 and role play with your teacher.

Read and match.

1 How are you?

2 What's your name?

3 Hello, I'm Mrs Smith.

a I'm Patrick.

b Hello, Mrs Smith.

c I'm fine, thanks.

Listen, point and repeat.

triangle   circle   square   rectangle   star   heart

 Listen and repeat. Then look at 6. Ask and answer.

 What is it?   It's a triangle.

Listen and repeat. Then play a game.

Is it a square?

No.

Is it a heart?

Yes!

1:08

 9 **Listen, point and repeat.**

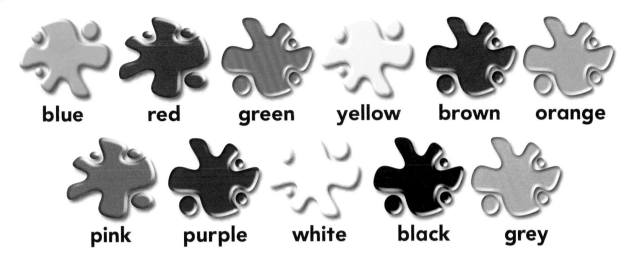

blue   red   green   yellow   brown   orange

pink   purple   white   black   grey

1:09

 10 **Listen and circle.**

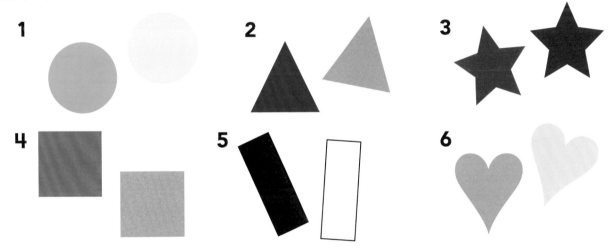

1   2   3

4   5   6

11 **Look at 10. Ask and answer.**

What colour is it?   It's blue. It's a blue circle.

1:10

 12 **Listen and repeat. Then ask the class.**

What's your favourite colour?

My favourite colour is green.

Name	Favourite colour

1:11

 13 **Listen, point and repeat.**

1	**2**	**3**	**4**	**5**
one	two	three	four	five
6	**7**	**8**	**9**	**10**
six	seven	eight	nine	ten
11	**12**	**13**	**14**	**15**
eleven	twelve	thirteen	fourteen	fifteen

1:12

14 **Count the shapes. Then listen and check.**

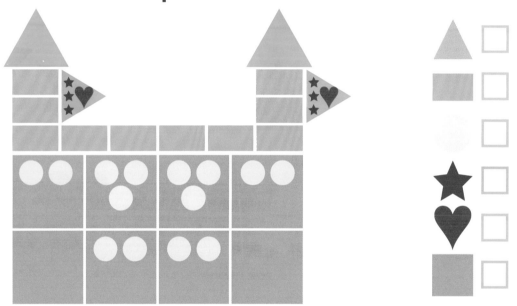

15 **Look at 14. Ask and answer.**

How many rectangles?　　Ten. Ten rectangles.

1:13

 16 **Listen and repeat. Then ask the class.**

How old are you?

I'm seven.

7

Name	Age

17 Listen and chant.

Listen to the Teacher!

Stand up!	Point to the window!	Pick up your pencil!
Stand up!	Point to the door!	Pick up your book!
Put up your hand	Clap your hands	Open your book
And turn around!	And sit down!	And close your book!

18 Listen and number.

a

b

c

d

19 Play the game.

Turn around!

Simon says "Turn around!".

Good Morning, Class!

1:17

1 Listen, look and say.

1 desk 2 book 3 crayon 4 rubber

5 marker pen 6 pen 7 pencil 8 ruler

9 chair 10 backpack

1:18

2 Listen, find and say. **3** Play a game.

4 **Listen and sing. Then look at 1 and find.**

The Classroom Song

Good morning, class.
Good morning to you!
How are you?
I'm fine, thank you.

What is it? It's a rubber.
What is it? It's a ruler.
What is it? It's a pencil.
What is it? It's a crayon.

Now pick up your pen
And open your book.
Say the words
And write with me.
Let's start now. 1, 2, 3!

Chorus

 5 **Listen and number.**

a    **b**    **c**    **d**

6 **Look at 5. Ask and answer.**

What is it?

It's a chair.

 **THINK BIG** **What is it? Listen, number and say.**
book ☐   backpack ☐   pencil ☐

song/vocabulary Unit 1 **11**

7 Listen and read. What colour is the marker pen?

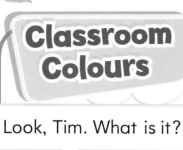

1

Look, Tim. What is it?

It's a pen.

2

Look! What are they?

They're pencils.

Yes, they're yellow pencils.

3

And what is it?

It's a marker pen.
A red marker pen.

Yes! Good, Tim.

4

And what are they?

They're rubbers.

And what colour are they?

8 Look at the story. Then circle.

1 a 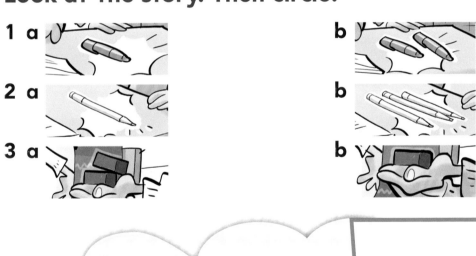   b

2 a   b

3 a   b

THINK BIG What happens next? Draw and say.

1:26

9 Listen. Help Tim and Jane make sentences.

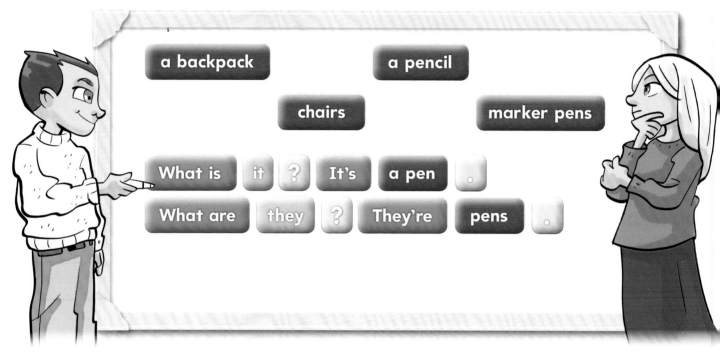

a backpack   a pencil

chairs   marker pens

| What is | it | ? | It's | a pen | . |

| What are | they | ? | They're | pens | . |

10 Circle and colour. Then circle and draw.

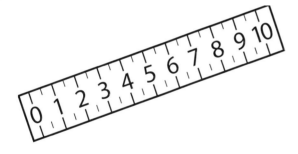

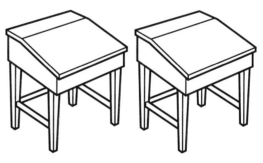

1 What is it? / What are they?
They're rulers. / It's a ruler.
It's blue. / They're blue.

2 What are they? / What is it?
It's a desk. / They're desks.
It's red. / They're red.

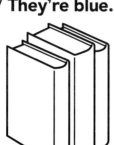

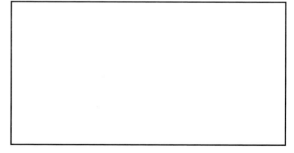

3 What is it? / What are they?
They're books. / It's a book.
It's yellow. / They're yellow.

4 What is it? / What are they?
They're rubbers. / It's a rubber.
It's brown. / They're brown.

1:28

11 Listen and stick. Then say.

1

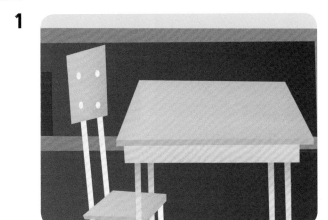

2

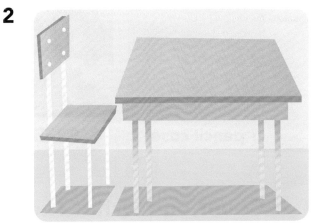

3

4

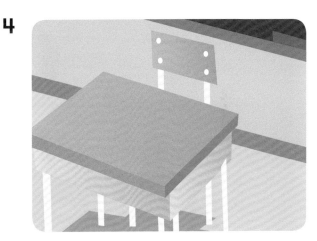

12 Look at 11. Ask and answer.

What is it?

What are they?

It's...

They're...

13 Draw and say.

14 Look, listen and repeat.

1 pencil case

2 tablet

3 pencil sharpener

4 notebook

 15 Count and write. Then listen and check.

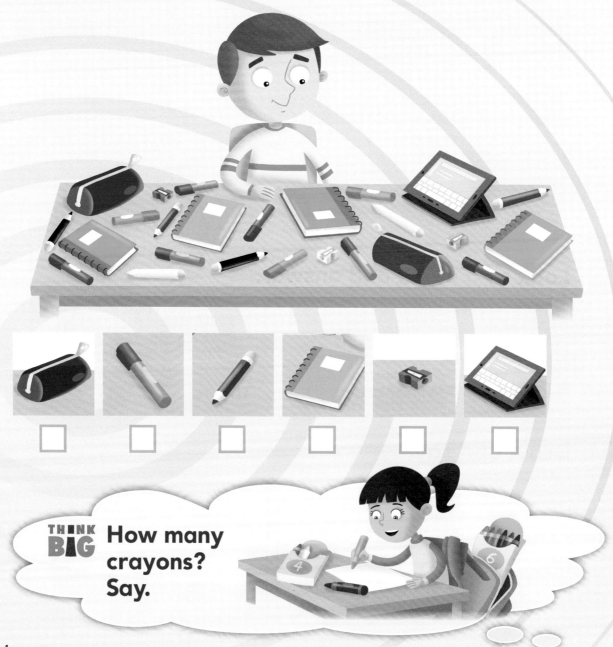

THINK BIG How many crayons? Say.

16 Listen and match.

1 Luke

2 Emma

3 Ahmed

a

b

c

17 Do a class survey.

	Me		
pencils			
notebooks			

How many pencils have you got?

I've got seven pencils.

PROJECT

18 Make a My Pencil Case poster. Then present it to the class.

My Pencil Case

I've got a blue pencil case. I've got...

1:32

Listen and find the picture. Then listen and repeat.

a

Please sit down.

Thank you.

b

Thank you.

You're welcome.

20 Look and number. Then say.

1 2 3 4

Thank you. ☐

Please sit down, Anna. ☐

Thank you, Susie. ☐

You're welcome. ☐

THINK BIG How can you be polite in class?

1:33

21 **Listen, look and repeat.**

1 a   **2** t   **3** p   **4** n

1:34

22 **Listen and find. Then say.**

pan   **ant**   **nap**   **tap**

1:35

23 **Listen and blend the sounds.**

1 a-n   an   **2** p-a-t   pat

3 p-a-n-t   pant   **4** t-a-n   tan

5 a-t   at

1:36

24 **Underline a, t, p and n. Then listen and chant.**

Pat the ant
Has got a tan.
Pat the ant
Takes a nap.

1:38

25 **Look and find the differences. Then listen and check.**

Picture A

Picture B

 1:39

26 **Listen and play a game.**

1:40

 27 **Listen and circle.**

1

2

3
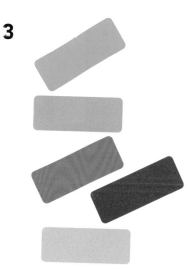

28 **Read and match.**

1 What is it?
It's a desk.

a
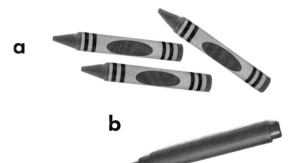

2 What are they?
They're pencil sharpeners.

b

3 What is it?
It's a marker pen.

c

4 What are they?
They're crayons.

d

I Can

☐ name classroom objects.

☐ talk about the things I've got.

☐ be polite.

My Family

1 Listen, look and say.

1:41

1 grandad
2 grandma
3 mum
4 dad
5 brother
6 sister
7 me
8 parents (mum and dad)
9 grandparents (grandma and grandad)

1:42

2 Listen, find and say. **3** Play a game.

4 **Listen and sing. Then look at 1 and find.**

My Family

My family, my family!
This is my family.
He's my brother
And she's my sister.

My dad, my mum!
My sister, my brother!
We have so much fun!
I love them.

My family, my family.
I love my family!
I love them
And they love me.
I love my family!

5 **Look at 4 and circle the correct answer.**

1 grandad / dad   2 grandma / sister
3 mum / brother   4 sister / brother

6 **Look at 4. Ask and answer.**

Who's he?

He's my grandad.

THINK BIG **Are all families the same?**
Who's in your family?

7 Listen and read. How many brothers? How many sisters?

A Big Family

And who's he?

He's my brother.

5

Patrick!

Yes, Patrick!

PHOTOS

6

8 Look at the story. Then circle.

1 She's my mum.

a  b

2 He's my dad.

a   b

3 They're my brother and sister.

a  b

THINK BIG Who's missing? Draw.

1:47

9 **Listen. Help Tim and Jane make sentences.**

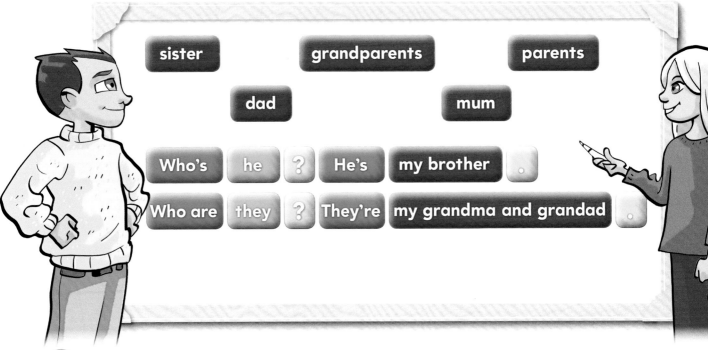

| sister | grandparents | parents |

| dad | mum |

Who's | he | ? | He's | my brother | .

Who are | they | ? | They're | my grandma and grandad | .

10 **Follow. Then draw and say.**

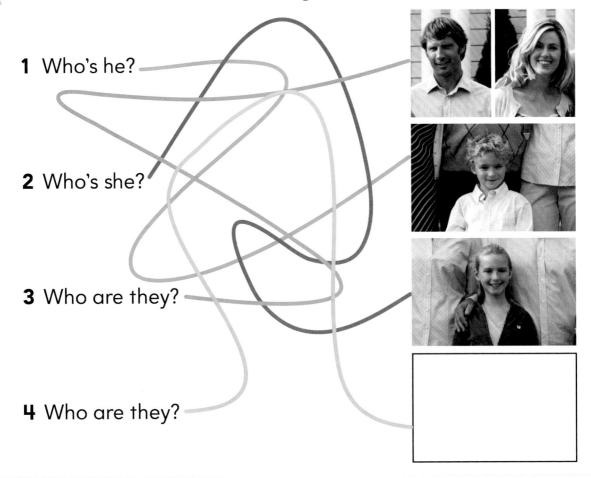

1 Who's he?

2 Who's she?

3 Who are they?

4 Who are they?

1:49

 Listen and stick. Then say.

1

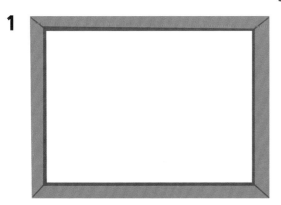

2

3

4

12 **Look at 11. Role play with a partner.**

How many brothers and sisters have you got?

I've got two sisters.

You're number...

13 **Draw and say.**

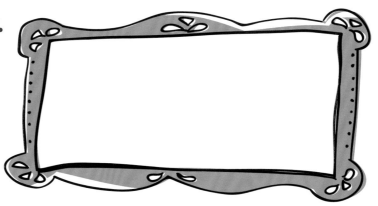

1:50

14 **Look, listen and repeat.**

1 boy

2 girl

3 man

4 woman

1:51

15 **Listen and find. Is the baby a boy or a girl?**

THINK BIG **Is your teacher a man or a woman?**
Is your best friend a boy or a girl?

1:52

16 Listen and number.

a

b

c

d

17 Work with a partner. Look at 16. Play a game.

This is my baby sister.

Yes.

Picture c?

18 Make a Family poster. Then say.

My Family

This man is my dad and this woman is my mum...

content connection (gender) Unit 2 **29**

1:53

19 **Listen and read. Then circle.**

Can I help you?

Yes, thank you.

1 Pam helps her **brother** / **sister**.

Please help me.

OK. I can help you.

2 Tommy helps his **brother** / **sister**.

20 **Can you help? Role play with a partner.**

THINK BIG Can you help your family? Can you help more?

21 Listen, look and repeat.

1 i   **2** s   **3** b   **4** d

 22 Listen and find. Then say.

sit   **in**   **dad**   **bat**

 23 Listen and blend the sounds.

1 i-s   is   **2** p-i-n   pin   **3** b-a-d   bad

4 d-i-p   dip   **5** s-a-d   sad   **6** i-t   it

 24 Underline i, s, b and d. Then listen and chant.

Don't sit, sit, sit
On a pin, pin, pin.
It's bad, bad, bad
To sit on a pin!

25 **Work with a partner. Ask and answer. Then draw.**

Who's in your family?

My mum and dad. I've got two sisters and I've got a brother.

26 **Play a game.**

27 **Listen and ✔.**

1 a  b  **2** a  b

3 a  b  **4** a  b

28 **Listen and number.**

a  b  c

I Can

- [ ] talk about my family.
- [ ] say how many brothers and sisters I've got.
- [ ] ask to help my family.

My Body

1:62

1 Listen, look and say.

1 head
2 eye
3 ear
4 nose
5 mouth
6 neck
7 hand
8 arm
9 finger
10 leg
11 foot
12 toe

1:63

2 Listen, find and say. **3** Play a game.

4 **Listen and sing. Then look at 1 and find.**

1:64 1:65

My Body Song

Have you got two ears?
Have you got one mouth?
Have you got two eyes?
Yes, I have. Yes, I have.

I've got ten fingers.
I've got ten toes.
I've got two feet
And one big nose!

And have you got long legs?
And have you got short hair?
And have you got small hands?
I sing my body song, my body song,
I sing my body song again!

1:66

5 **Listen and ✓.**

1 a  b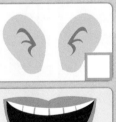

2 a  b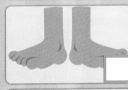

3 a b

6 **Look at 5. Ask and answer.**

How many ears have you got?

I've got two ears.

THINK BIG **Have you got short or long hair? Who do you know who's got short or long hair?**

1:68

7 **Listen and read. What's the teddy bear's name?**

Lost Teddy

1. Have you got a teddy bear?

   I don't know. Let's see.

   Bobo...

2. Is this your teddy bear?

   No. My teddy bear has got small ears.

3. Is this your teddy bear?

   No. My teddy bear has got short legs.

4. Is this your teddy bear?

   No, my teddy bear is brown.

8 Look at the story. Circle Bobo.

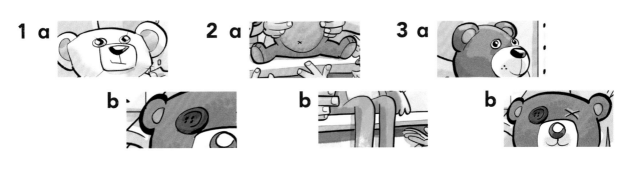

1 a   2 a   3 a

b   b   b

THINK BIG What's your favourite toy? What does it look like? Draw and say.

1:69

9 Listen. Help Tim and Jane make sentences.

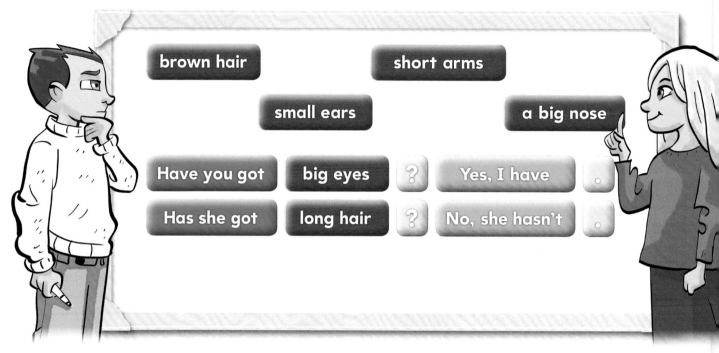

brown hair   short arms

small ears   a big nose

| Have you got | big eyes | ? | Yes, I have | . |
| Has she got | long hair | ? | No, she hasn't | . |

10 Read and circle. Draw and say.

1 Has she got short hair?
Yes, she has. / No, she hasn't.

2 Has he got long legs?
Yes, he has. / No, he hasn't.

3 Has it got small ears?
Yes, it has. / No, it hasn't.

4 Has your grandad got white hair?
Yes, he has. / No, he hasn't.

1:71
11 Listen and stick. Then say.

1   2

3   4

12 Look at 11. Ask and answer.

I've got a long neck.

Have you got long arms?

No, I haven't.

Are you number...?

13 Draw and say.

14 **Look, listen and repeat.**

1:72

1 see   **2 smell**   **3 taste**   **4 hear**

1:73

15 **Listen, circle and read.**

1 I see with my **ears** / **eyes**. I see a

 photo .

2 I taste with my **mouth** / **nose**. I taste

 cake .

3 I hear with my **neck** / **ears**. I hear a

 guitar .

4 I smell with my **nose** / **head**. I smell a

 flower .

THINK BIG **Can you see, hear, taste or smell these things?**

16 Circle T for true and F for false.

1 I smell with my mouth.   **T**   **F**

2 I see with my eyes.   **T**   **F**

3 I taste with my nose.   **T**   **F**

4 I hear with my ears.   **T**   **F**

5 I smell with my nose.   **T**   **F**

17 Draw and say.

1 I see

2 I smell

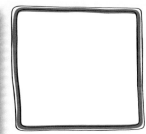

cake   flower   guitar
ice cream   photo   song
star   teddy bear   TV

3 I taste

I see with my eyes. I see a star.

4 I hear

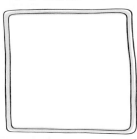

PROJECT

18 Make a My Senses poster. Then present it to the class.

My Senses

I hear...   I see...   I taste...   I smell...

I taste pizza.

content connection (the senses) Unit 3 **41**

1:74

19 **Listen and number. Then listen and repeat.**

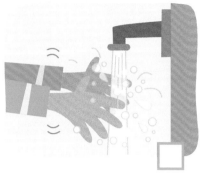

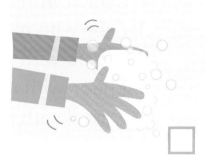

Rinse with water.   Dry your hands.   Wash with soap.

1:75 1:76

20 **Listen and circle. Then match and sing.**

Keep Clean

1 Every day
Before I eat
And after I play
I **dry / wash** my hands.

2 With a lot of soap
It's easy, you see.
Rinse / Dry with water
Just like me.

3 **Dry / Wash** them well and
Sing this song.
Keep your hands clean
All day long!

a

b

c

THINK BIG **Do you wash your hands before you eat? Why?**

21 **Listen, look and repeat.**

1 e   **2** c   **3** g   **4** m

 22 **Listen and find. Then say.**

cap   **map**   **pen**   **gas**

 23 **Listen and blend the sounds.**

1 p-e-t   pet   **2** c-a-t   cat   **3** g-e-t   get
4 m-a-t   mat   **5** w-i-g   wig

 24 **Underline e, c, g and m. Then listen and chant.**

The cap is on the cat.
The cat goes on the map.
The pen goes on the bed.

25 **Complete the monster. Listen, draw and colour.**

26 **Draw your own monster. Ask and answer with a partner.**

 How many heads has it got?

It's got three heads!

1:84

27 Listen and ✔.

1 a   b   2 a   b

3 a   b   4 a   b

28 Look and write.   fingers   foot   hand   toes

1 _____   2 _____   3 _____   4 _____

I Can

☐ name parts of the body.

☐ talk about my senses.

☐ say how I keep clean.

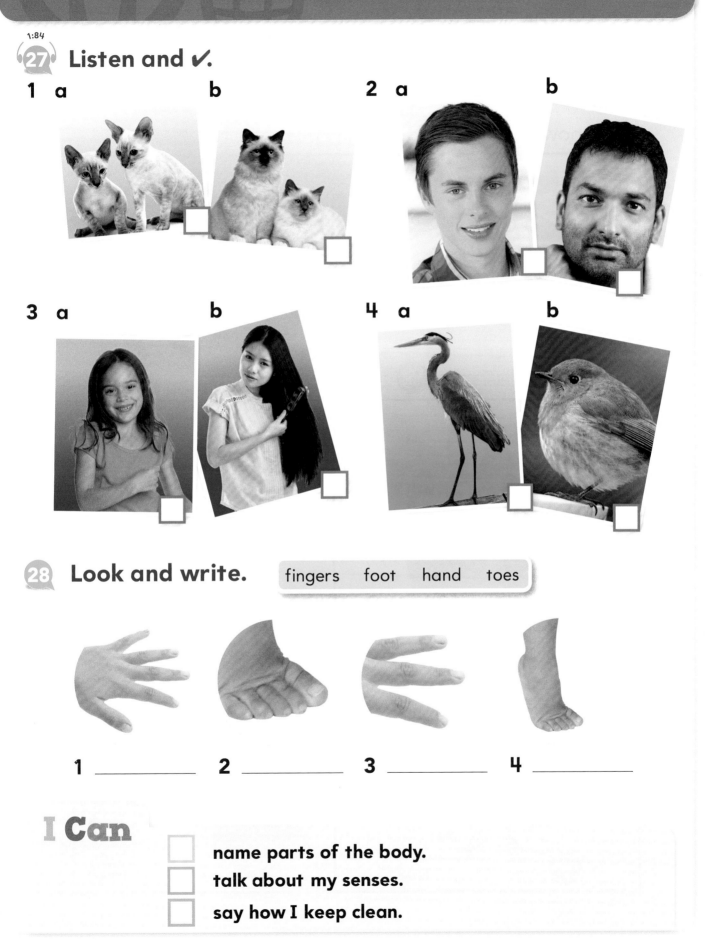

Do I Know It?

1 Look and circle. Practise.

☺ I know this.   ☹ I don't know this.

1:85 1:86

2 Get ready.

A Listen and number.

B Look at **A** and point. Ask and answer.

What is it?   It's a backpack.

C Listen and circle.

1 Mark

2 Kate

D Look at **C** and point. Role play with a partner.

Who's she?   She's my sister.

3 Get set.

 Cut out the cards on page 139.
Now you're ready to **Go!**

1:87

4 Go!

A Listen. Put the cards on the numbers.

1	2	3

4	5	6

B Point to a card. Ask and answer.

Card 2. Has she got long hair?   Yes, she has.

5 Write and draw.

All About Me

My name is: _____

This is me.

This is my family.

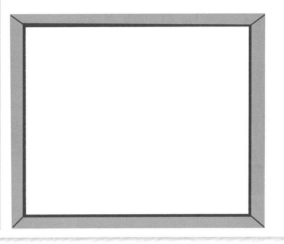

Do I Know It Now?

6 Think about it.

A Go to page 46. Look and circle again.

B Tick (✔).

☐ I can start the next unit.

☐ I can ask my teacher for help and then start the next unit.

☐ I can practise and then start the next unit.

7 Rate this Checkpoint. Colour the stars.

 easy hard

 fun not fun

unit 4
My Favourite Clothes

2:01

1 Listen, look and say.

1 boots　　**2 dress**　　**3 gloves**　　**4 hat**　　**5 jacket**

6 trousers　　**7 blouse**　　**8 shoes**　　**9 skirt**

10 T-shirt　　**11 socks**　　**12 shirt**　　**13 shorts**

2:02

2 Listen, find and say.　　**3** Play a game.

4 **Listen and chant. Then look at 1 and find.**

What Are You Wearing?

What are you wearing?
I'm wearing a T-shirt.
What are you wearing?
I'm wearing a skirt.

What's he wearing?   What's she wearing?
He's wearing new shorts.   She's wearing a red hat.
What's he wearing?   What's she wearing?
He's wearing old boots.   She's wearing pink shoes.

2:05

5 **Listen and number in order.**

a  b  c   d

e   f  g   h

6 **Point, ask and answer.**

What is it?

It's a pink T-shirt.

THINK BIG **Look, think and say the clothes.**

2:07

7 **Listen and read. What colour is Patrick's hat?**

My Favourite Hat!

What are you wearing?

I'm wearing a green hat. It's my favourite hat.

1

2

What's Tim wearing?

He's wearing a brown hat. It's his favourite hat.

3

What's Maria wearing?

She's wearing a purple hat. It's her favourite hat.

4

8 Look and match.

1    **2**    **3**    **4**

a   **b**    **c**   **d**

THINK BIG Draw a funny hat. Then show the class.

2:08

9 **Listen. Help Tim and Jane make sentences.**

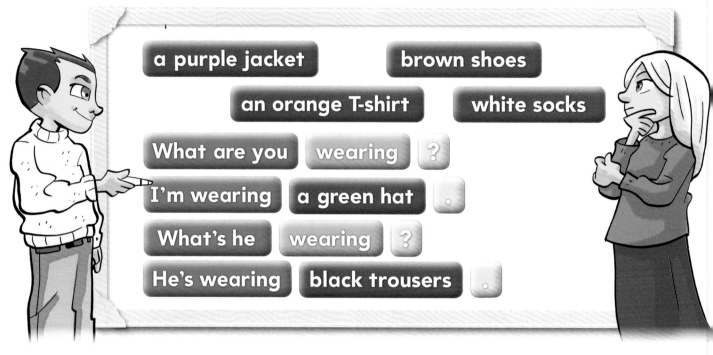

a purple jacket   brown shoes

an orange T-shirt   white socks

What are you | wearing | ?

I'm wearing | a green hat | .

What's he | wearing | ?

He's wearing | black trousers | .

10 **Match. Then say. Use He's wearing or She's wearing.**

1   2   3   4

a   b   c   d

2:10

11 **Listen and stick. Then say.**

12 **Role play with a partner.**

What are you wearing?

I'm wearing an orange T-shirt...

13 **What are you wearing? Draw and say.**

2:11

14 **Look, listen and repeat.**

1 **hot**   **2** **wet**   **3** **cold**   **4** **dry**

5 **mountains**   **6** **desert**   **7** **jungle**

2:12

15 **Listen and read. Is it wet in the desert?**

1 It's cold in the mountains. I'm wearing my hat and gloves.

2 It's wet in the jungle. I'm wearing my jacket and boots.

3 It's hot and dry in the desert. I'm wearing my shorts and hat.

THINK BIG **Draw and say.**

16 Read and circle. Then say.

1 It's   in the mountains. I'm wearing a .

2 It's   in the desert. I'm wearing a .

3 It's   in the jungle. I'm wearing a .

17 Look at 15. Play a game.

What are you wearing?

I'm wearing a hat. It's cold.

You're number 1.   Yes.

18 Make a Clothes poster. Then present it to the class.

My Clothes

It's hot in the jungle. I'm wearing a dress.

2:13

 Listen and number. Then say.

a

b

c

They're wearing traditional clothes from Guatemala.

They're wearing traditional clothes from the Philippines.

They're wearing traditional clothes from Kenya.

20 **Look at 19. Ask and answer.**

What are they wearing?

They're wearing big hats and blue dresses.

THINK BIG Do people wear traditional clothes in your country? What do they wear?

21 **Listen, look and repeat.**

1 o   **2** k   **3** ck

 22 **Listen and find. Then say.**

kid   **sock**   **on**

 23 **Listen and blend the sounds.**

1 p-o-t   pot   **2** k-i-t   kit   **3** n-e-ck neck
4 k-i-ck kick   **5** d-o-g   dog   **6** p-i-ck pick

 24 **Underline o, k and ck. Then listen and chant.**

Put on your socks,
Put on your kit.
Kick the ball,
Kick, kick, kick!

25 **Work in two pairs. Ask and answer.**

What's Emily wearing?

She's wearing a green blouse and brown trousers.

What's Michael wearing?

He's wearing a blue jacket and black trousers.

26 **Work in two groups. One group looks away and answers the teacher. Score 1 point for each correct answer.**

What's Antonio wearing?

He's wearing a yellow T-shirt and blue trousers.

Take turns. Which group remembers the most?

2:19

27 **Listen and ✔.**

1 a  ☐ b ☐ c ☐

2 a ☐ b ☐ c ☐

3 a ☐ b ☐ c ☐

4 a ☐ b ☐ c ☐

28 **Look and write.**

| boots | jacket | shirt | trousers |

1 _____ 2 _____ 3 _____ 4 _____

I Can

☐ say what people are wearing.

☐ talk about clothes.

☐ respect all cultures.

unit 5

Busy at Home

1 Listen, look and say.

1 brushing my teeth

2 drinking

3 combing my hair

4 reading

5 having a bath

6 making lunch

7 washing

8 getting dressed

9 sleeping

10 playing

11 talking on the phone

12 eating

2:22

2 Listen, find and say.   **3** Play a game.

4 Listen and sing. Then look at 1 and find.

What Are You Doing?

I'm brushing my teeth.
I'm combing my hair.
I'm busy. I'm busy.
What are you doing?

I'm eating my breakfast.
I'm washing my face.
I'm busy. I'm busy.
What are you doing?

I'm talking on the phone.
I'm making my lunch.
I'm busy. I'm busy.
What are you doing?

Chorus

5 Listen and say yes or no.

1    2    3

6 Look at 5. Ask and answer.

What are you doing?

I'm eating.

You're Number 1!

THINK BIG Why do we brush our teeth?
Why do we get dressed?

2:27

7 **Listen and read. What's Patrick drawing?**

Fun at Home

What are you doing, boys?

We're playing.

1

What are you doing, Mum?

I'm talking on the phone!

2

What are you and Patrick doing?

I'm reading and he's reading, too.

That's good.

3

Boys, I'm making lunch.

4

8 Look at the story. Circle.

1 Who is playing?

2 Who is making lunch?

3 Who is drawing?

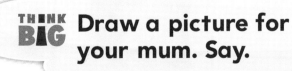

THINK BIG Draw a picture for your mum. Say.

2:28

9 **Listen. Help Tim and Jane make sentences.**

getting dressed   sleeping

having a bath   drinking

What are you   doing   ?

I'm   talking on the phone   .

What's she   doing   ?

She's   washing   .

2:29

10 **Listen and ✔. Then say.**

1 What's she doing?
a   b

2 What's he doing?
a   b

3 What's he doing?
a   b

4 What's she doing?
a   b

2:31

11 **Listen and stick. Then say.**

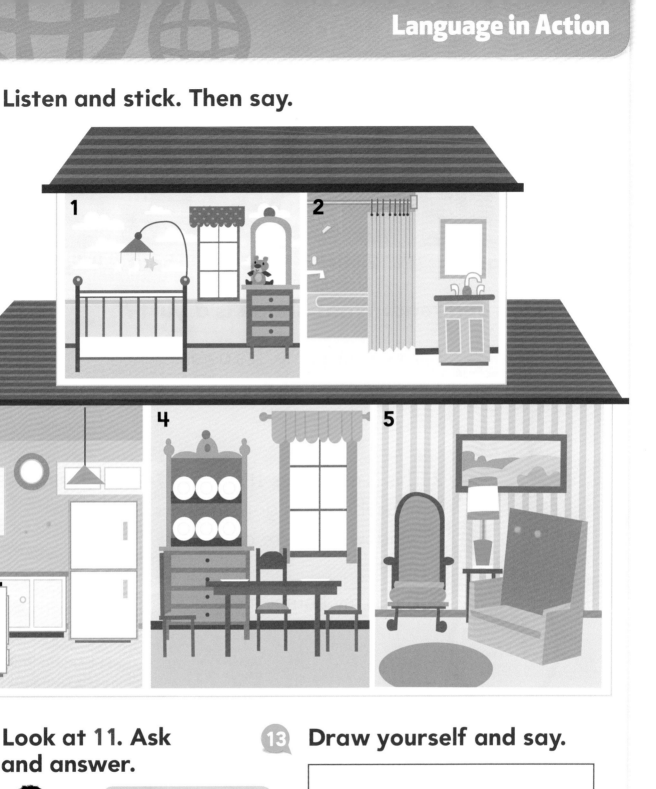

12 **Look at 11. Ask and answer.**

13 **Draw yourself and say.**

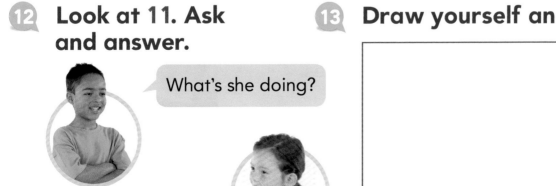

What's she doing?

She's sleeping.

language practice (*What's she doing? She's sleeping.*) Unit 5 **67**

2:32

 Look, listen and repeat.

1 flat   **2 yurt**   **3 houseboat**   **4 lighthouse**

2:33

 Listen and read. What shape is a yurt?

1 This is my home. It's a yurt. It's a circle.

2 This is my home. It's a houseboat. It's got small windows. They're circles.

3 This is my home. It's a lighthouse. It's got a big door.

4 This is my home. It's a flat. It's got big windows. They're rectangles.

THINK BIG Find a picture of one of these homes. What shapes can you see?
a igloo   **b** hut   **c** teepee

16 **Listen and number.**

a  ☐

b  ☐

c 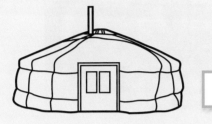 ☐

d  ☐

17 **Look at 16. Play a game.**

It's got four windows.
They're triangles.

Yes.

It's Number 3.
It's a houseboat.

18 **Make a House Shapes poster. Then present it to the class.**

My house is a square.
It's got two windows.
They're circles...

2:35

 19 **Listen and match. Then listen and repeat.**

She's helping her parents.
She's drying the dishes.

She's cleaning her room.
He's washing the dishes.

1

2

3

4

20 **How do you help at home? Act it out. Your partner guesses.**

He's drying the dishes.

THINK BIG **Does it feel good to help at home? Why?**

2:37

21 **Listen, look and repeat.**

1 u   **2** f   **3** ff

2:38

22 **Listen and find. Then say.**

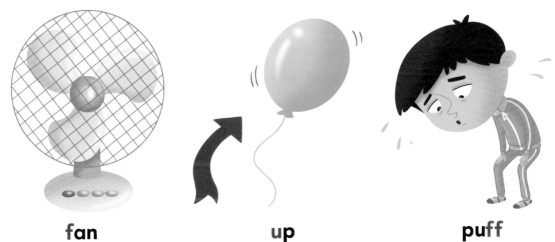

fan   **up**   **puff**

2:39

23 **Listen and blend the sounds.**

1 r-u-n   run   **2** f-u-n   fun   **3** o-ff   off
4 s-u-n   sun   **5** f-o-g   fog

2:40

24 **Underline u, f and ff. Then listen and chant.**

We're having fun,
Running in the sun.
Up, up, up!
Puff, puff, puff!

25 Work in groups. Play the Memory game.

Pupil 1: Act and say.

Pupil 2: Talk about Pupil 1. Then act and say.

Pupil 3: Talk about Pupils 1 and 2. Then act and say.

Play with the whole class. How much can you remember?

2:42

26 **Listen and number.**

a

b

c

d

e

27 **Look and circle.**

1

2

3

4

1 He's **making lunch / eating**.
3 She's **getting dressed / sleeping**.

2 She's **combing her hair / having a bath**.
4 She's **drinking / reading**.

I Can

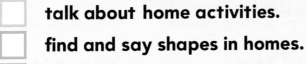

- talk about home activities.
- find and say shapes in homes.
- talk about helping at home.

unit 6

On the Farm

2:43

1 Listen, look and say.

1 cat

2 dog

3 cow

4 sheep

5 turtle

6 horse

7 duck

8 frog

9 chicken

10 goat

2:44

2 Listen, find and say.　　**3** Play a game.

4 Listen and chant. Then look at 1 and find.

2:45 2:46

Look at the Animals

Look over here!
Look over there!
There are animals
Everywhere!

What is it?
It's a duck.
What's it doing?
It's flying up high!

What is it?
It's a dog!
What's it doing?
It's jumping with the frogs!

What are they?
They're goats!
What are they doing?
They're eating some oats!

Chorus

2:47

5 Listen and number.

a

b

c

6 Look at 5. Ask and answer.

What is it?

It's a horse.

What's it doing?

It's running.

THINK BIG What animals can jump?
What animals can fly?

2:49

7 **Listen and read. What's the goat doing?**

It's Eating Your Skirt!

Is that your cat?

Yes, it is.

What's it doing?

It's jumping.

What's the duck doing?

It's flying.

What are the chickens doing?

They're running.

8 Look and number.

1 running   **2** flying   **3** eating   **4** jumping

a

b

c

d

THINK BIG What happens next? Draw.

2:50

9 **Listen. Help Tim and Jane make sentences.**

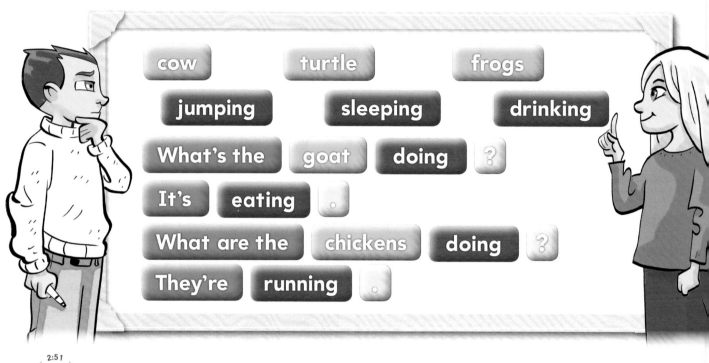

cow   turtle   frogs

jumping   sleeping   drinking

What's the   goat   doing   ?

It's   eating   .

What are the   chickens   doing   ?

They're   running   .

2:51

10 **Listen and ✔.**

1 a   b   2 a   b

3 a   b   4 a   b

2:53

11 **Listen and stick. Then say.**

12 **Look at 11. Ask and answer.**

 What's the horse doing?

It's eating.

13 **Colour and say. What are the animals doing?**

2:54

14 **Look, listen and repeat.**

1 chick   2 puppy   3 kitten   4 calf

2:55

15 **Listen and read. What is a baby cat called?**

1 A baby cow is called a calf. This cow is big. This calf is small.

2 A baby dog is called a puppy. Look at this dog. She's got puppies.

3 A baby chicken is called a chick. This chicken is big. These chicks are small.

4 A baby cat is called a kitten. Look at this cat. She's got kittens.

THINK BIG **Read and match.**

chick   kitten   puppy   calf

dog   chicken   cow   cat

2:56

16 Listen and number. Then say.

a

A baby chicken is called a...

b

A baby dog is called a...

c

A baby cat is called a...

d

A baby cow is called a...

17 Look at 15. Ask and answer.

What are baby dogs called?

Baby dogs are called puppies.

PROJECT

18 Make a Baby Animals poster. Then present it to the class.

Baby Animals

a kitten

a calf

a puppy

A baby cat is called a kitten...

2:57

 19 **Listen and find the picture. Then listen and repeat.**

1 feeding

2 walking

3 brushing

4 playing

20 **Look at 19. Role play with a partner.**

What are you doing?

I'm feeding the chicks.

THINK BIG How are you kind to animals? Draw.

2:59

 21 **Listen, look and repeat.**

1 r   **2** h   **3** j

2:60

 22 **Listen and find. Then say.**

hat   **jam**   **rock**

2:61

 23 **Listen and blend the sounds.**

1 r-e-d red   **2** h-e-n   hen   **3** j-e-t   jet
4 r-u-n run   **5** h-u-t   hut   **6** j-o-b   job

2:62

 24 **Underline r, h and j. Then listen and chant.**

A red hen in
A red hat
Is eating red jam.
Run, red hen, run!

2:64

25 **Listen, find and say. Then role play.**

1

2

3

4

26 **Work in teams. Role play. Ask and answer.**

What's the dog doing?

It's jumping.

27 **Look and match.**

a

b

1 eating

2 flying

3 jumping

4 running

c

d

2:65

28 **Listen and number.**

a

b

c

d

29 **Read and circle.**

1 A baby dog is called a
chick / puppy.

2 A baby cow is called a
kitten / calf.

3 A baby chicken is called a
calf / chick.

4 A baby cat is called a
puppy / kitten.

I Can

☐ name animals and baby animals.

☐ talk about what animals are doing.

☐ say how to be kind to animals.

1 Look and circle. Practise.

☺ I know this.   ☹ I don't know this.

2:66

Get ready.

A Look. Circle the correct words.

1 Mum is **reading a book** / **eating**.

2 Dad is **washing** / **making lunch**.

3 The cat is **sleeping** / **playing**.

4 The girl is **drinking** / **talking on the phone**.

B Look at **A** and point. Ask and answer.

What's she wearing?

She's wearing a green shirt and brown trousers.

C Listen and number.

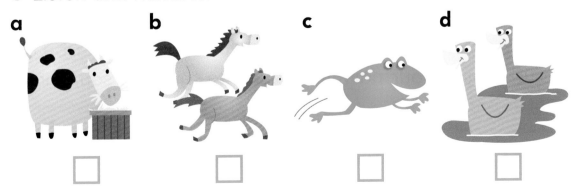

a □ **b** □ **c** □ **d** □

3 Get set.

STEP 1 Cut out the cards on page 141.

STEP 2 Put the cards on your desk. Mix the cards up. Now you're ready to **Go!**

4 Go!

A Arrange the cards to make the person below. Ask and answer with a partner.

- What's she wearing?
- What's she doing?

B Make 3 more people. Don't show your cards. Describe one of your people. Your partner makes the same person. Show your cards and check.

He's in the bathroom. He's talking on the phone...

5 **Draw.**

All About Me

My favourite animal is:

I'm wearing:

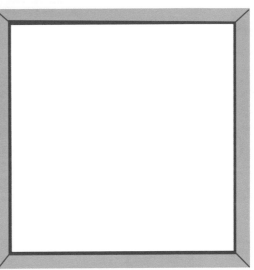

Do I Know It Now?

6 **Think about it.**

A Go to page 86. Look and circle again.

B Tick (✔).

☐ I can start the next unit.

☐ I can ask my teacher for help and then start the next unit.

☐ I can practise and then start the next unit.

7 **Rate this Checkpoint. Colour the stars.**

easy   hard

fun   not fun

Party Time

3:01

1 Listen, look and say.

1 cake

2 fruit

3 ice cream

4 juice

5 milk

6 water

7 pizza

8 salad

9 chicken

10 chips

11 pasta

3:02

2 Listen, find and say.

3 Play a game.

4 Listen and sing. Then look at 1 and find.

It's My Party!

Welcome, friends.
Please sit down.
It's time for my party!
With games and a clown!

I've got pizza, chicken,
Salad, too.
Fruit, cake
And ice cream for you!

Or put some pasta
On your plate.
With juice or milk
It sure tastes great.

Thanks for the presents.
What a great day!
Let's eat and drink
And play, play, play. (x2)

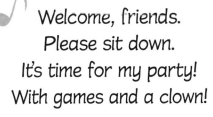

5 Listen and say yes or no.

1
2
3
4

6 Look at 5. Ask and answer.

What's he got?

He's got milk.

THINK BIG **What food do you eat every day?**
What food do you eat on special days?

song/vocabulary Unit 7 **91**

3:07

7 **Listen and read. What day is Tim's party?**

8 **Look at the story. Read and circle.**

1 Tim's got...

a  b

2 Jane's got...

a  b

3 What's Patrick got?

a  b

THINK BIG **What day is it today? Circle and say.**

Monday Tuesday Wednesday Thursday Friday Saturday Sunday

3:08

9 Listen. Help Tim and Jane make sentences.

water

fruit

chicken

milk

What   have you got   ?

I've got   salad   .

What   has she got   ?

She's got   juice   .

10 Match. Then say.

1 What have you got?
I've got salad.

2 What have you got?
I've got cake and milk.

3 What have you got?
I've got juice and ice cream.

4 What have you got?
I've got fruit.

a

b

c

d

3:09

11 Listen and stick. Then say.

12 Look at 11. Ask and answer.

What's she got?

She's got fruit.

13 What have you got? Draw and say.

3:10

14 Look, listen and repeat.

1 sugar

2 chocolate

3 biscuits

4 salt

5 crisps

6 chips

 3:11

15 Listen and read. Is chocolate sweet or salty?

1 This is sugar. It's sweet.

2 Chocolate, cake and biscuits are sweet, too.

Sweet   *Salty*

Pure White Sugar

3 This is salt. It's salty.

4 Crisps, pizza and chips are salty, too.

 THINK BIG **Name other sweet and salty foods. What's your favourite? Salty or sweet?**

16 Look and match. Then listen and check.

sweet   salty

17 Look at 16. Play a game.

Ice cream...

Ice cream is sweet! Crisps...

Crisps are salty!

PROJECT

18 Make a Sweet and Salty Food poster. Then present it to the class.

sweet   salty

Chocolate is sweet. Chips are salty.

3:14

 19 **Look and number in order. Then listen and check.**

a

I eat lunch
every day.

b

I eat dinner
every day.

c

I eat breakfast
every day.

20 **Read and match. Then draw and say.**

1 My brother eats salad for lunch
every day.

a

2 Mum drinks milk for breakfast
every day.

b

3 Dad eats chicken for dinner
every day.

c

4 I eat...

d

THINK BIG **Do you eat three meals every day?
Why do you think it is important?**

21 Listen, look and repeat.

1 l   **2** ll   **3** v   **4** w

22 Listen and find. Then say.

web   **doll**   **leg**   **van**

23 Listen and blend the sounds.

1 l-e-t   let   **2** b-e-ll   bell   **3** v-e-t   vet
4 w-e   we   **5** w-i-n   win   **6** t-a-ll   tall

24 Underline l, ll, v and w. Then listen and chant.

Let's ring the bell
For the vet
With the van!

3:20

25 **Find the differences and say. Then listen and check.**

Picture A

Picture B

26 **Look at 25. Play a game.**

In Picture A, Sam's got ice cream.

In Picture B, Sam's got fruit.

3:22

27 **Listen and circle.**

1
  a
  b
  c

2
  a
  b
  c

3
  a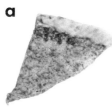
  b
  c

4
  a
  b
  c

28 **Read and match.**

1 Chips   **a** is sweet.
2 Biscuits   **b** is salty.
3 Juice   **c** are salty.
4 Chicken   **d** are sweet.

I Can

☐ **talk about party food.**
☐ **ask and answer about what people have got.**
☐ **name sweet and salty food.**

unit 8 Fun and Games

3:23

1 🎧 Listen, look and say.

1 action figure

2 plane

3 ball

4 bike

5 blocks

6 cars

7 stuffed animal

8 doll

9 game

10 puppet

11 train

3:24

2 🎧 Listen, find and say.   **3** 💬 Play a game.

4 **Listen and sing. Then look at** 1 **and find.**

What's in Your Toy Box?

Kim, what's in your toy box?
Have you got a plane?
No, but this is my blue car.
And where's my grey train?

Kim, what's on your toy shelf?
Have you got a ball?
Yes, yes, here it is.
And here's my purple doll.

Kim, what's on your table?
Have you got big blocks?
Yes, and these are my puppets.
My favourite's Mr Fox!

These are my favourite toys,
Purple, green and grey.
I share my toys with my friends.
And I play every day!

3:28

5 **Listen and number.**

a    b    c

6 **Look at** 5. **Ask and answer.**

What's in your toy box?

These are my blocks.

THINK BIG **What toys can a baby play with? Why?**
What toys can big children play with? Why?

7 **Listen and read. Where is Jane's doll?**

8 Look at the story and circle.

1 Jane's doll is under the

a   b .

2 Jane's action figures are on the

a   b .

3 Jane is playing with her

a   b .

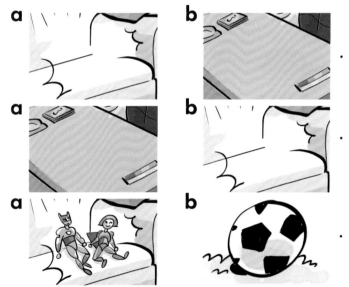

THINK BIG What's your favourite toy?
Where is your favourite toy?

3:31

9 Listen. Help Tim and Jane make sentences.

on the shelf under the table

plane stuffed animals

Where's the ball ?

It's in the toy box .

Where are the blocks ?

They're under the sofa .

3:32

10 Listen and ✔.

1
a b

2
a b

3
a b

4
a b

3:33

11 **Listen and stick. Then say.**

12 **Look at 11. Ask and answer.**

Where are the dolls?

They're under the table.

13 **Colour and say.**
Where are the toys?

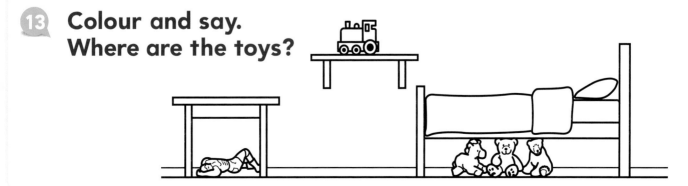

language practice (*Where are the dolls? They're under the table.*) Unit 8 **107**

3:34

 14 **Look, listen and repeat.**

| **1 kite** | **2 fish** | **3 dragon** | **4 bird** | **5 butterfly** |

3:35

 15 **Listen and read. What colour is the dragon kite?**

1 This kite looks like a dragon.
It's red, black and yellow.

2 This kite looks like a bird.
It's blue and orange.

3 This kite looks like a butterfly.
It's green.

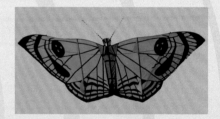

4 This kite looks like a fish.
It's orange.

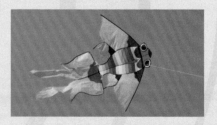

THINK BIG **Find a picture of a kite. What colour is it? What does it look like?**

3:36

16 Listen and number. Then colour.

a
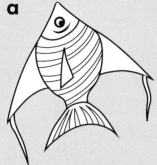

b

c

d

☐   ☐   ☐   ☐

17 Look at 16. Play a game.

> It's red. It looks like a dragon.

> Number 1.

PROJECT

18 Make a Cool Kite. Then present it to the class.

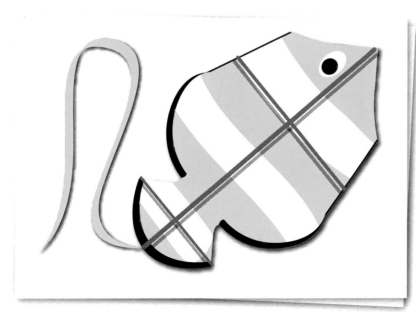

> My kite looks like a fish. It's yellow.

3:37

 19 **Listen and find the picture. Then listen and repeat.**

1

2

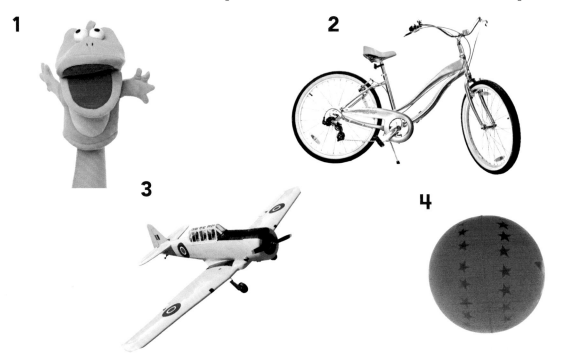

3

4

20 **Look and number. Then say.**

a

b

c

Sharing is fun!

Here's my car.
Let's share.

Okay. Thank you!

THINK BIG **Is it good to share your toys?
Why?**

3:38

21 **Listen, look and repeat.**

1 qu   **2** x   **3** y

3:39

22 **Listen and find. Then say.**

yell   quick   six

3:40

23 **Listen and blend the sounds.**

1 qu-a-ck   quack   **2** b-o-x   box   **3** y-e-s   yes
4 o-x   ox   **5** f-o-x   fox   **6** y-u-m   yum

3:41

24 **Underline qu, x and y. Then listen and chant.**

Six quick foxes,
In a yellow box!

3:43

25 **Listen and circle. Then say.**

26 **Look at 25. Ask and answer.**

Where are the action figures?

They're on the bed and under the chair.

Where are the planes?

They're on the shelf and under the desk.

27 Look and match.

1 blocks

2 bike

3 cars

4 game

5 puppet

6 train

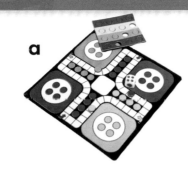
a

b

c

d

e

f

28 Look and circle. Then say.

1 It looks like a
fish / dragon.
It's...

2 It looks like a
butterfly / bird.
It's...

3 It looks like a
dragon / butterfly.
It's...

I Can

☐ **name toys.**

☐ **say where something is.**

☐ **talk about sharing my toys.**

Play Time

3:45

1 Listen, look and say.

1 catching

2 throwing

3 hitting

4 kicking

5 dancing

6 singing

7 skating

8 riding

9 skipping

3:46

2 Listen, find and say.   **3** Play a game.

4 **Listen and sing. Then look at 1 and find.**

Play Time Is Cool!

We like play time at our school.
Skipping and dancing,
Throwing and catching.
Play time is cool at our school!

I'm throwing the ball.
It's so much fun!
Are you
Hitting and running?
Yes, and it's fun.

We're kicking the ball
And trying to score.
It's so much fun.
Let's play some more.

Chorus

5 **Listen and ✔.**

1 a    **b**    **2 a**    **b**

6 **Look at 5. Ask and answer.**

Are you kicking?

Yes, I am.

THINK BIG **Look at 1. What are they doing with their feet? What are they doing with their hands?**

3:51

7 **Listen and read. What's Ann doing?**

I'm Not Tired!

1
Hi, Ann.

Hi, Mrs Smith.

2
Thanks for babysitting, Ann. Is Tim sleeping?

No, he isn't, Mrs Smith.

3
Is Patrick sleeping?

No, he isn't. He's jumping on the bed.

4
Tim! Patrick! Let's go to bed!

I'm not tired!

I'm not tired!

8 Look at the story. Number the pictures in order.

a 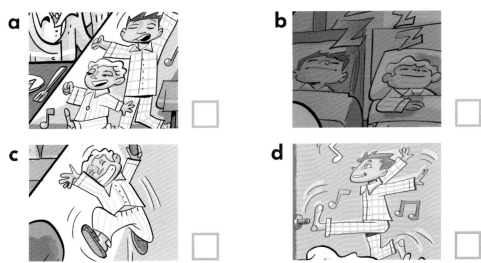 ☐

b ☐

c ☐

d ☐

THINK BIG Imagine you are getting ready for bed. Act it out and say what you are doing!

3:52

9 Listen. Help Tim and Jane make sentences.

skipping   throwing

skating   riding

Is she | singing | ?

Yes, she is | .

Are they | dancing | ?

No, they aren't | .

3:53

10 Listen and number.

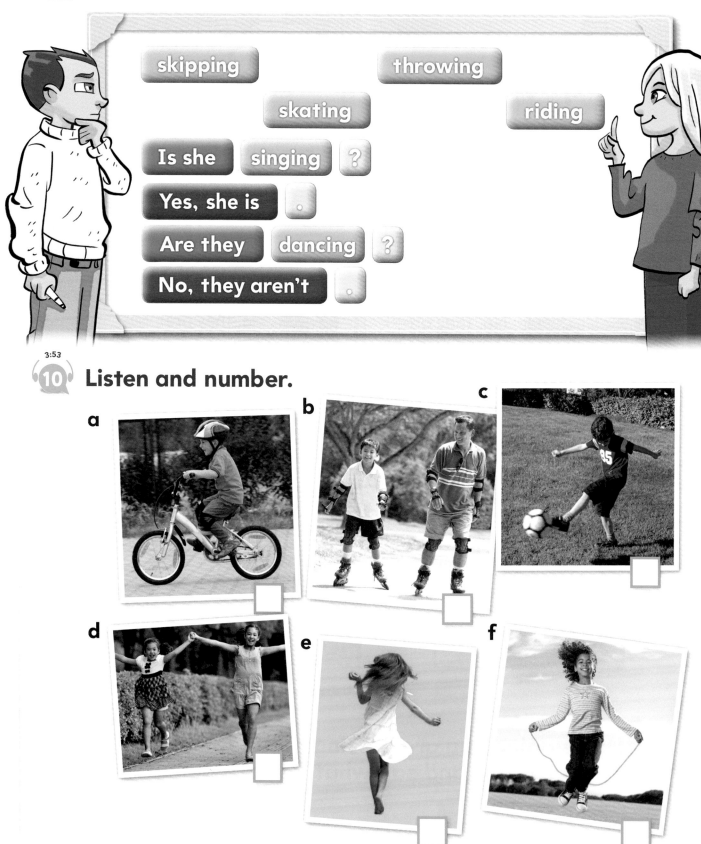

a

b

c

d

e

f

3:54

11 Listen and stick. Then say.

12 Look at 11. Ask and answer.

Is she running?

No, she isn't.
She's skipping.

13 Draw and say. Are you throwing a ball?

3:56
14 **Listen, repeat and find.**

3:57
15 **Listen and read. Who's counting?**

climbing

1 Let's climb! Are you climbing to the top?

skipping

2 Let's skip! Jump! Jump!

In the playground

hide and seek

3 Let's play hide and seek. I'm counting. 1, 2, 3...

hopscotch

4 Let's play hopscotch! I've got number two. I'm hopping!

tag

5 Let's play tag! Are you running?

THINK BIG **What do you do in the playground? What are your three favourite games?**

16 **Read and number. Then listen and check.** 3:58

a Let's play tag! ☐

b Let's skip! ☐

c Let's play hopscotch! ☐

d Let's play hide and seek! ☐

e Let's climb! ☐

17 **Look at 16. Play a game.**

Let's skip!

PROJECT

18 **Make a Play Time poster. Then present it to the class.**

Play Time

Hopscotch

Let's play tag!

3:59

19 **Listen and find the picture. Then listen and repeat.**

1

2

3

3:60

20 **Listen and number. Then say.**

a

Get enough exercise.

b

Get enough sleep.

c

Get enough food and drink.

THINK BIG **How do you look after your body?**

21 **Listen, look and repeat.**

1 SS   **2** Z   **3** ZZ

 22 **Listen and find. Then say.**

buzz   **kiss**   **zip**

 23 **Listen and blend the sounds.**

1 m-e-ss mess   **2** z-a-p zap   **3** f-i-zz fizz
4 m-i-ss miss   **5** j-a-zz jazz

 24 **Underline ss, z and zz. Then listen and chant.**

Buzz goes the bee.
Zip, zap!
It misses me!

3:66

25 Listen and circle.

26 Look at 25. Ask and answer.

Is he skipping?

Yes, he is.

Are they jumping?

No, they aren't. They're running.

3:67

27 **Listen and number.**

a

b

c

d

e

f

28 **Read and match.**

1 Let's play tag.

2 Let's climb.

3 Let's play hide and seek.

4 Let's skip.

5 Let's play hopscotch.

a

b

c

d

e

I Can

☐ talk about actions people are doing.

☐ talk about games children play.

☐ say how I look after my body.

1 **Look and circle. Practise.**

🙂 I know this. 🙁 I don't know this.

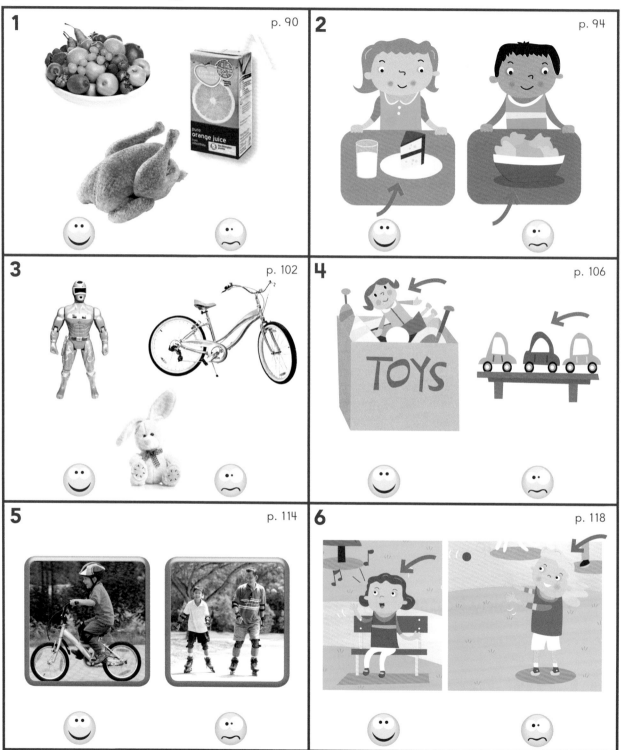

3:69 3:70

2 Get ready.

A Look. Listen to the questions. Circle the correct words.

1 It's on the **shelf** / **table**.
2 They're **on** / **under** the bed.
3 Yes, **he** / **she** has.

B Listen again and check. Then practise with a partner.

C Look at **A**. Answer these questions with a partner.

  1 What food can you see? What drinks can you see?

  2 How many toys can you see? What are they?

  3 What day is it?

3 Draw.

STEP 1 Cut out the outline on page 143.

STEP 2 Fold the paper to make a book.

STEP 3 Write in your book. Colour the front.
Now you're ready to **Go!**

4 Go!

A Read your book with three classmates. Take turns.
Write the presents.

Classmate	Present
Bruno	a train
1	
2	
3	

B Look at your books. Answer these questions with a partner.
  1 Page 2: What are they doing?
  2 Page 3: What food and drink have they got?
  3 Page 3: Where's the cat?
  4 Page 4: How many presents can you see?

5 **Draw.**

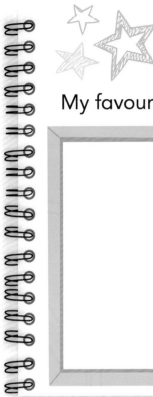

All About Me

My favourite food is:

My favourite toy is:

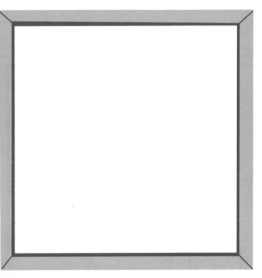

Do I Know It Now?

6 **Think about it.**

A Go to page 126. Look and circle again.

B Tick (✔).

☐ I can ask my teacher for help.

☐ I can practise.

7 **Rate this Checkpoint. Colour the stars.**

easy   hard

fun   not fun

– 5 questions –

3:71

Look at the picture. Now listen and look. There is one example.

– 5 questions –

Look at the pictures. Now listen and look. There is one example.

Young Learners English Practice Starters: Listening C

– 5 questions –

3:73

Look at the pictures. Now listen and look. There is one example.

What's she wearing?

A ✔   **B** ☐   **C** ☐

1   Is your brother eating?

A ☐   **B** ☐   **C** ☐

2   What's she doing?

A ☐   **B** ☐   **C** ☐

3 What are they?

A ☐

B ☐

C ☐

4 What are the cats doing?

A ☐

B ☐

C ☐

5 What are his favourite clothes?

A ☐

B ☐

C ☐

– 5 questions –

**Look and tick. Put a tick (✔) or an (✗) in the box.
There are two examples.**

Examples

This is a chair. ✔

This is a ruler. ✗

Questions

1

This is a baby. ☐

2

This is a foot. ☐

3

This is a book. ☐

4

This is a sister. ☐

5

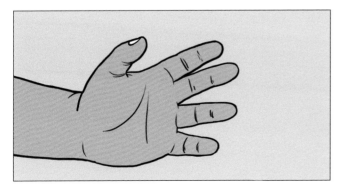

This is a hand. ☐

– 5 questions –

Look and read. Write *yes* or *no*.

Examples

The farmer is wearing boots.	yes
The dog is running.	no

Questions

1	The girl is feeding the ducks.	_____
2	The chickens are eating.	_____
3	The girl has got short hair.	_____
4	The boy is reading a book.	_____
5	The farmer has got a red shirt.	_____

Young Learners English Practice Starters: Reading & Writing C

– 5 questions –

Look at the pictures. Look at the letters. Write the words.

Example

t r a i n   a r n t i

Questions

1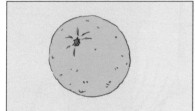

_ _ _ _ _ _   g n a o e r

2

_ _ _ _ _ _   t p u p e p

3

_ _ _ _ _   l a d s a

4

_ _ _ _ _ _   t a k s e s

5

_ _ _ _ _ _ _ _   d i n s h c a w

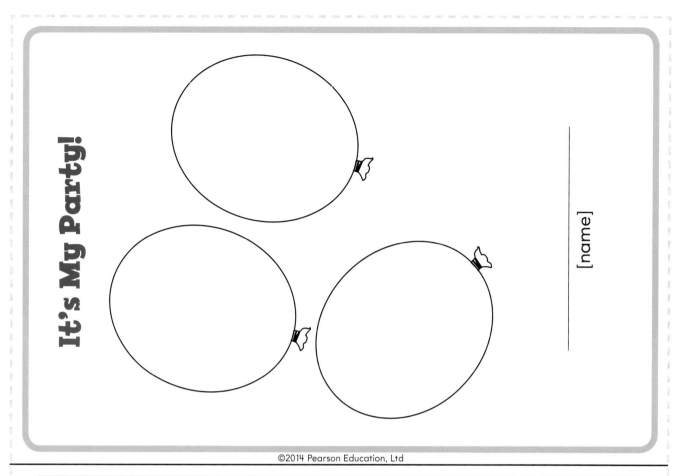

It's My Party!

_____
[name]

I've got a present. It's a
_____ . I'm happy today!
[toy]

4

Today is _____ [day] _____.

I'm having a party.

2

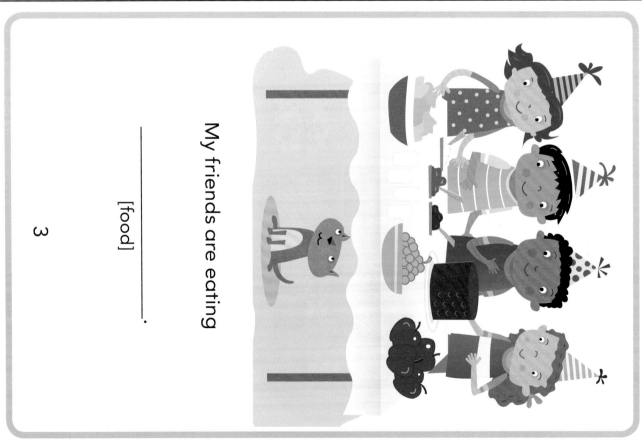

My friends are eating _____ [food] _____.

3